TAKING A STAND

WHAT GOD CAN DO THROUGH ORDINARY YOU!

HOWARD G. HENDRICKS

MULTNOMAH PRESS
PORTLAND, OREGON 97266

Design and photography by Walvoord, Killion, Edmondson & Hanlon, Inc.

TAKING A STAND
© 1972, 1983 by Howard G. Hendricks
Published by Multnomah Press
Portland, Oregon 97266

Printed in the United States of America

First Printing 1983

Library of Congress Cataloging in Publication Data
_____

Hendricks, Howard G.
    Taking a stand.

    Rev. ed. of: Elijah; confrontation, conflict, and crisis. 1972.
    1. Elijah, the prophet.   I. Title.
BS580.E4H45   1983   248'.4   83-8241
ISBN 0-88070-025-4 (pbk.)

CONTENTS

INTRODUCTION

Have you ever wondered why there is so much in the Scriptures that is biographical? It is obvious to even a casual reader of this Book that its pages are permeated with personality—men and women who are not fugitives from a wax museum but who are made of the same tissue of life as each of us. The Holy Spirit loves to teach truth taken from life.

Spiritual biographies leave us in *admiration*. I cannot come away from the life of a man like Abraham, Moses, Barnabas, or Paul without my spiritual tongue hanging out. I know some say, "You can lead a horse—or a person—to water, but you can't make him drink." That's right. But you can feed him salt. And the lives of godly men and women in the Scriptures are the salt that the Spirit often uses to make us hungry and thirsty for righteousness.

Studying biblical biographies leaves us *without excuse*. I find it tears away every excuse that I palm off to God as a reason why I am not living more effectively for him.

Finally, such a study leaves us with *hope*. Don't say, "It can't be done." They did it.

Some years ago I had a deacon in my church who was the reincarnation of Peter. Every week that went by, I was more convinced that Peter had returned in the flesh. In a Bible class I had a series on the life of Peter, and I brought the series

> *"The life of this early day prophet is a primer, a rudimentary set of instructions for the child of God facing a heathen world."*

to a climax by using the thumbnail sketch our Lord made of the apostle Peter in John 1:42: " 'You are Simon son of John. You will be called Cephas' (which, when translated, is Peter [rock])." The before and the after. When I got to the end, everybody got up and walked out except this man. He sat directly in front of me with his head cupped in his hands, looking directly at me.

Finally he said, "Preacher, I've got it."

"You've got what, Jack?"

"I've got it. If God can do something for Peter, he can do something for me."

God the Spirit was speaking loud and clear through an individual with whom this man could identify.

The life of Elijah is another biblical example that the Spirit of God can use to teach us truth.

Elijah. His name means "Yahweh is God!" He exploded into the dismal pagan northern kingdom of Israel like a divine exclamation point. From his abrupt entrance onto the stage of King Ahab's playpen of idolatry to his stirring whirlwind departure into heaven, the fire of Elijah purged and healed and enlightened the wayward Hebrew nation. His flaming spirit pulsated through the prophets and into the New Testament. With Elijah-like fervor, John the Baptist announced the arrival of the Lamb of God who would take away the sin of the world. He appeared with Moses on the Mount of Transfiguration in conversation with our Lord.

Lest we perceive him as larger than life, however, James cautions: "Elijah was a man just like us. He prayed. . . ." The life of this early day prophet is a primer, a rudimentary set of instructions for the child of God facing a heathen world.

Like holding five symbolic fingers in the air, Elijah's biblical portrait hoists a hand of warning from God against tolerating sin and depending on man. The prophet combines incredible strength and almost pathetic vulnerability. He displays an unassailable faith and distressing cowardice. He is, as James said, just like us.

COURAGE IN CONFRONTATION

*I*n this study I would like to emphasize five
episodes in the life of Elijah: confrontation
with King Ahab, communion with God,
conflict with the prophets of Baal, communication from God, and the crisis experience of commitment following failure.

> Now Elijah the Tishbite, from Tishbe in
> Gilead, said to Ahab, "As the Lord, the
> God of Israel, lives, whom I serve, there
> will be neither dew nor rain in the next
> few years except at my word" (1 Kings
> 17:1).

Up the palace steps, into the presence of King
Ahab, storms the irate prophet. I think I overhear
two of the secret service men. One says to the
other, "Hey! Where did he come from? How did
he get in here?" And while they're discussing the
matter, Elijah has disappeared.

Whence such courage? You will never understand nor appreciate what Elijah did until you
understand the times in which he lived. The nation was on the skids. There was a mania of
mediocrity. Seven thousand believers were
huddled miserably in a cave in silent protest:
"We don't want to get involved." This man,
Elijah, stands out like a spiritual colossus in the
midst of a generation of perverts and spiritual
pygmies. Chapter 16 tells the sad story of the

rapid spread and universal prevalence of idolatry. It comes to a climax in verses 30-33:

> Ahab son of Omri did more evil in the eyes of the LORD than any of those before him. He not only considered it trivial to commit the sins of Jeroboam son of Nebat, but he also married Jezebel daughter of Ethbaal king of the Sidonians, and began to serve Baal and worship him. He set up an altar for Baal in the temple of Baal that he built in Samaria. Ahab also made an Asherah pole and did more to provoke the LORD, the God of Israel, to anger than did all the kings of Israel before him.

"It was not convenient nor comfortable to take a stand for God in that generation. It never is."

It was not convenient nor comfortable to take a stand for God in that generation. It never is. What is the secret of a man or a woman communicating with a generation of chaos? May I underscore in your thinking three keys, three secrets, to the effective communication of this man in his generation and to effective communication in our generation?

In the first place, Elijah was convinced of the reality of Jehovah. "As the LORD, the God of Israel, lives. . . ." He's alive. Ahab and those confederate with him thought they had successfully embalmed and interred Jehovah-worship. But they made one serious miscalculation: They forgot a man. And that's all it takes in any generation with the living God—one man overwhelmed by His aliveness, shot through with the reality only God can bring into human experience.

The most convincing thing about Christianity is its power to change men. The world is not overwhelmed by your argumentation. The world is convinced only by that which it cannot produce—reality in human experience. Only God can produce that. That's why Christianity is the most revolutionary thing in the world; it promises to revolutionize people.

What is there in your life that you cannot explain on any basis other than the supernatural? What is there in your life that is proof positive of the reality of God in your life? So you believe God is alive. Why, there's not an unbeliever in a carload. I didn't ask you if you believed that. I asked you what changes are being wrought in your experience today that are proof positive to a world screaming for reality that God is alive?

It is amazing how difficult it is for the Lord to break through to us in certain areas. I used to pray for years as a father, "Lord, change my children." And nothing happened.

Then I began to see that my prayer must be changed: "Lord, change my children's father." And when God was pleased to do that, I saw remarkable, dramatic changes in my children.

Some years ago I was to speak at a banquet on a Friday night and then, the following morning, catch a plane for a weekend ministry. As I came home from the seminary and drove into the driveway, my headlights fell upon my boy's bicycle tire—flat as a doornail. I knew it was either now or never; so I plowed in and we fixed Bob's bicycle tire. I got washed up and tore across town, and got to the banquet about twenty minutes late.

The emcee had ulcers on his ulcers by the time I got there.

"Where in the world have you been?"

"I'm awfully sorry," I said. "I had a flat."

"I thought you had a new car."

"I do. It was my boy's bicycle tire."

Boom! This man's cork went off, and, quite frankly he gave me a portion of his mind he could ill-afford to lose. After he got through, I said to him (graciously, I hope), "Did it ever occur to you, my friend, that on certain occasions it is far more important that I fix my boy's bicycle tire than that I eat your meal?"

Sometime later my boy and I were out in the park playing ball together, and then we took a little walk through a wooded section. We stopped under a tree and were throwing some stones into a creek and I asked him, "Hey, Bob, do you love me?"

"I sure do, Dad."

"Great. Why?"

". . . what changes are being wrought in your experience today that are proof positive to a world screaming for reality that God is alive?"

11

"Why? I don't know."

"Bob, you never want to love anybody or anything without having a reason."

It must have been a half hour later when he spun around and said, "Hey, Dad! I've got a reason!"

"A reason for what?" (Quite frankly, I had forgotten all about our earlier conversation.)

"Why I love you."

"Oh, wonderful, pal. Why?"

"Because you play ball with me and fix my bicycle tire."

Did you ever have the Lord pick up a two-by-four and drop it right on the center of your head?

My children are not impressed by the fact that I'm a seminary professor. They are impressed by the reality of Jesus Christ in my life. It would be easy in this book to pull the wool over your eyes, but it's not easy to pull the wool over the eyes of my wife and those in my family. They know whether I have the real disease or not.

How do you convince a world that God is alive? By his aliveness in your life, by his work in producing reality in your experience. What a message for a phony generation.

I want you to notice a second truth in Elijah's experience that I believe the Spirit of God wants to weave into the pattern of ours. Not only was he convinced of the reality of Jehovah, he was also convinced that he was a representative of the living God: "As the LORD, the God of Israel, lives, whom I serve. . . ." My friends, that gives dignity to Christian experience. I never cease to be amazed that God can consistently perform the miracle of the ministry; that is, to employ human personality to accomplish his purpose. I am a personal representative of the living God.

In the midst of a generation screaming for answers, Christians are stuttering. Christians are paralyzed. Christians are uninvolved in giving the only answer to the searching questions which men are asking. And I know many Christians are asking, "What can I do?" I am quite sure that Elijah could have come to the same conclusion: The nation is headed for doom. The moral microbes are eating the heart out of it.

It is still true, as in Elijah's time, that God is looking for one man, one woman, who will become his personal representative. Behind the pulpit? Certainly. In a classroom in a Bible school? By all means. Through varied forms of Christian work? To be sure. But also in communities, in homes, in offices, in shops, on university and college and high school campuses, where people who are blind to the glories of our Christ see him incarnate in you, his personal representative.

My spiritual experience has been revolutionized recently. I must confess, as many a Christian worker must, that it's very easy to become compulsively active. It is hard to learn the lesson of the barrenness of busyness. Activity simply becomes an anesthetic to deaden the pain of an empty life. And if we get off long enough, we discover we have activity without accomplishment. I used to get up every morning with the compulsiveness of a Christian: "I've got to go to work today. I've got to witness today. I've got to do this and that today." I was quite active, but there was a sterility about my experience. Then the truth dawned on me that all God wanted for me was to be available—his messenger boy, a suit of clothes in his ready-to-wear department that he could put on at will to accomplish his purpose.

I once had a week of meetings in which I spoke thirty-four times in eight days. Right after the meetings I flew from Chicago to Los Angeles with a plane change in Denver. By the time we got to Denver, I was weary. When I got on the plane, I went all the way to the back—third seat in—hoping no one would come and sit by me. "Lord, don't send anyone here. Your servant has been so busy." The plane filled up and nobody sat there, until finally the only seat left was the one next to me. A man got on the plane, came down the aisle, sat down next to me, took out his little executive case, opened it, and then with expletives I shall not repeat, shouted, "Where is my brief? I'm on my way to try a case in Los

"It is still true, as in Elijah's time, that God is looking for one man, one woman, who will become his personal representative."

Angeles and I don't have the brief." He got up, tore down the aisle, and told the stewardess, "You've got to open that door. I've got to get out of here." So they went through all the pains of opening the door.

Sitting outside, now completely exhausted and partially asleep, was a GI who had been bumped nineteen times in a row—and this was the nineteenth. The agent said, "Hey, buddy, you're on." He never got the message. He told me later they had to almost pick him up and put him on the plane. And this boy came down the aisle and sat next to me.

I thought, *Lord, I hope he's not talkative.* He was incurably talkative. Finally, in the midst of the conversation, he asked, as invariably someone will, "By the way, sir, what do you do?"

This is always embarrassing. I usually make good progress in conversation until somebody asks, "Oh, by the way, what do you do?"

"Well, I'm in education."

"Oh, that's very interesting. Where do you teach?"

"Well, I teach at the Dallas Theological Seminary."

"The what? Oh, yeah! I get it, you're a preacher!"

"Yes, I'm a preacher."

"Sir, I'm on my way to Vietnam. I know I'm not supposed to be, but I'm scared to death. You got anything that would help me?"

So I got my Testament out and explained the gospel to him, and somewhere between Denver and Los Angeles, he accepted Christ as his Savior. I said, "Now, friend, I want you to do me a favor. I'm going to write my name and address on this card. When you get to Vietnam, I want you to drop me a note, and I'll send you some literature that'll help you build on this foundation."

So this guy got to Vietnam, and when he walked into the barracks, the sergeant said, "Hey, buddy. You new around here?"

"Yes, sir."

"OK, I want you to get the signals straight. Tomorrow's Sunday, and in this outfit everybody goes to chapel. That includes you. Right?"

"Yes, sir."

So Sunday he went to chapel, and the chaplain got up and preached the gospel. The kid thought, *You know, that's the same thing that guy talked about on the plane.* So after the service he went up to talk to the chaplain.

"Hey, chaplain, an amazing thing happened. I was flying from Denver to Los Angeles and a man told me the very same thing you were talking about, and I received Jesus Christ as my Savior. In fact, he said that if I'd write to him, he'd send me some literature. Here's his name."

And the chaplain said, "That was my professor at Dallas Seminary."

A lot of people would say, "Isn't that an interesting story? Isn't that filled with coincidences?" A lawyer just happened to forget his brief; a kid just happened to be bumped nineteen times in a row; he just happened to sit down next to me; he just happened to ask if I could help him with his fear; he just happened to land in Vietnam, and of all the places, in a group where there was a believing chaplain who preached the Word of God and got him in a Bible class so that he could grow. I don't believe that any of this was coincidence at all. I believe this is a part of the excitement of waking up every day to say, "Lord, I'm simply your suit of clothes. Put me on to accomplish your purpose."

I want you to see one final truth. Elijah was not only convinced of the reality of Jehovah and that he was a personal representative of God to his generation; but he was also convinced of the resources which were available to him.

We need to do some reconstructing of the text, and in the book of James you will find a divine commentary on this passage. In James 5:17 we are told something that we know nothing about in 1 Kings: "Elijah was a man just like us. He prayed earnestly that it would not rain, and it did not rain on the land for three and a half years."

This man's courage to confront the king and his generation was the product of his prayer life.

"Lord, I'm simply your suit of clothes. Put me on to accomplish your purpose."

> *"Oh, for the capacity to stretch ourselves out upon an infinite God and to believe him to do what he specializes in: The impossible."*

But where did he get the idea to pray like that? Two verses in Deuteronomy 11 give us a clue, I think:

> Be careful, or you will be enticed to turn away and worship other gods and bow down to them. Then the LORD's anger will burn against you, and he will shut the heavens so that it will not rain and the ground will yield no produce, and you will soon perish from the good land the LORD is giving you (vv. 16-17).

It is my personal conviction that Elijah knew that what God had promised, he was able also to perform. He knew that God had promised that if a nation defected spiritually, he would withhold the rain. This man prayed earnestly that what God had promised, he would also perform.

So often people ask me, "What can I do? What resources are available to me in the midst of this apostasy?" Elijah did not have one thing that is not completely available to everyone reading this book. He had the Word of God. He had the power of prayer. What more do you need? The ability to believe God for what he says and then to appropriate it by believing prayer. It is one thing to believe the Lord, to know that he can do it, but it's quite a different thing to appropriate it in your experience.

I did something last summer I do not believe I have ever done before in my life. I hope I never have to do it again. I was in a prayer meeting made up just of pastors, and the unbelief was so crass I had to get up and walk out. I went back to my room and got the Word and filled myself with the living God until I realized afresh that I am his representative in this generation and that all the resources available to any other individual of faith are completely available to me.

There are too many black crepes hung on doors of Christian hearts, too many unbelievers. Oh, for the capacity to stretch ourselves out upon an infinite God and to believe him to do what he specializes in: The impossible.

COMMUNION
WITH GOD

*C*had Walsh wrote an intriguing book entitled *Early Christians of the Twenty-first Century*, in which he placed a burr in my mental saddle with these words:

> Millions of Christians live in a sentimental haze of vague piety, with soft organ music trembling in the lovely light from stained-glass windows. Their religion is a pleasant thing of emotional quivers, divorced from the will, divorced from the intellect and demanding little except lip service to a few harmless platitudes. I suspect that Satan has called off his attempt to convert people to agnosticism. After all, if a man travels far enough away from Christianity, he is liable to see it in perspective and decide that it is true. It is much safer, from Satan's point of view, to vaccinate a man with a mild case of Christianity so as to protect him from the real disease.

There is nothing as repulsive as phoniness in the spiritual realm. Conversely there is nothing as magnetic as reality. How refreshing to study the life of a man (Elijah) who was for real. There is not a shred of phoniness in this man's life and experience. Problems? Yes. Phoniness? No.

In the last chapter we focused our attention on

"You show me an individual who is communicating with his generation spiritually, and I will show you a man who is communicating with his God."

1 Kings 17:1, which constitutes an introduction to the life of the prophet. There we saw Elijah in confrontation. This rustic renegade from the rural regions storms into the palace of the king and delivers his ultimatum. He was able to communicate in a generation of spiritual decline because he was convinced of the reality of God—God was alive. He was also convinced that he was God's personal representative to that society, and that created responsibility, a responsibility to speak when others were hiding. Further, he was convinced that there were resources adequate and available. And the Word of God had become his word. He had laid hold of the throne of God in prayer, that it might not rain, and it rained not.

Now we turn from Elijah in confrontation to a study of Elijah in concealment. And there is a cause-effect relationship. You show me an individual who is effective in public, and I will show you an individual who is effective in private. You show me an individual who is communicating with his generation spiritually, and I will show you a man who is communicating with his God. We like the assignment of confrontation, but the assignment of concealment is hard to choke down.

May I encourage you to write four words in the margin of your Bible? These four words unravel the plot of 1 Kings 17:2-7. First, beside verses 2 and 3 write "command." Beside verse 4 write "promise"; beside verses 5 and 6, "response"; and beside verse 7, "test." The order is both significant and spiritual: a command, a promise, a response, and a test. Let's examine these in detail.

Note the command: "Then the word of the LORD came to Elijah: 'Leave here, turn eastward and hide in the Kerith Ravine, east of the Jordan' " (17:2-3).

"Hide myself, Lord? When there's so much to be done, and so few people involved in doing it? Hide myself?" Go show yourself. That's easy. Go hide. That's difficult. I'm sure, had I been in Elijah's place, I would have remonstrated with the Lord. "Lord, are you sure the IBM card is not crumpled? Lord, are you sure your PBX operator does not have the wrong plug in? Lord, I'm a palace man. And you want a palace man to hide himself?"

I am convinced that there are many Christians today to whom God is saying incisively, "Go hide yourself." That is a difficult assignment in a busy world. We are compulsive activists, and there are so many voices clamoring for our attention that it is easy to miss the voice of God. You may be asking God to use you, to shape you, to mold you, to give you a cutting edge, not only in this present generation but, if the Lord tarries, in the next. But you will have nothing to say to this generation or the next unless God first speaks to you.

The important thing is not what you read or what you hear in a school or in a conference from an individual who is simply an instrument in the hands of God. In the final analysis, the important thing is whether you hear from God himself. And if you do not hear from him, then all that those men and women may tell you will not make sense, nor will it have its designed impact.

At a pastors' conference some time ago I talked to a man who came to see me for counsel. He had severe problems in his work. I asked, "Pastor, how much time do you spend thinking?" "Thinking? Hendricks, I don't have any time to think. If I stop to think, I get behind."

This is precisely our dilemma.

During the fourth century, Julian the Apostate was determined to blot out every trace of Christianity. He discovered to his embarrassment the law of spiritual thermodynamics—the greater the heat, the greater the expansion. The more he persecuted Christianity, the more it flourished. Finally he gathered his little straggling band of men in an upper room and shouted to them, "Bah! Christianity provokes too much thinking. Why, even the slaves are thinking." This, to a Roman mind, was incredible. Slaves do not think. But slaves do think under the impact of the Word.

"We are compulsive activists, and there are so many voices clamoring for our attention that it is easy to miss the voice of God."

> "God never gives a command without providing the dynamic to fulfill that command."

Do you? I have never met a Christian who sat down and planned to live a mediocre life. But if most of us keep going in the direction we're moving, we may land there. The unexamined life is not worth living. How we need to hear in our giddy age, "Go hide yourself."

Now note the promise. God never gives a command without providing the dynamic to fulfill that command. He never calls you to a task without providing all the resources you need to accomplish it. " 'You will drink from the brook, and I have ordered the ravens to feed you there' " (17:4). Very simple fare, but sufficient.

I have wonderful opportunities working with students. One student who comes to see me periodically is now a young man dreaming dreams and seeing visions. If I can just keep him away from some older Christians who want to throw a wet blanket on what God is leading him to do, you're going to hear from this young man in the next generation. If I were to tell you what he is planning, many of you would laugh, so absurd appears to be his idea. But he feels God is leading him to it, he has been planning and thinking and praying. He came to see me not too long ago and said, "Prof, there are a lot of problems. God's going to have to do a miracle work if we ever get this off the ground."

I said, "That's what God specializes in. Did it ever occur to you that there is not a work of God in our day that has not been the product of a miracle-working God?" I reminded this student of the experience of Dallas Seminary.

Shortly after the seminary was founded in 1924, it almost folded. It came to the point of bankruptcy. All the creditors were going to foreclose at twelve noon on a particular day. That morning the founders of the school met in the president's office to pray that God would provide. And in that prayer meeting was Harry Ironside. When it was his turn to pray, he prayed in his characteristically refreshing manner: "Lord, we know that the cattle on a thousand hills are Thine. Please sell some of them and send us the money."

While they were praying, a tall Texan in boots and an open-collar shirt came into the business office. "I just sold two carloads of cattle in Fort Worth. I've been trying to make a business deal go through and it won't work, and I feel God is compelling me to give this money to the seminary. I don't know if you need it or not, but here's the check." A little secretary took the check and, knowing something of the critical-ness of the hour financially, went to the door of the prayer meeting and timidly tapped. When she finally got a response, Dr. Chafer took the check out of her hand, and it was for the exact amount of the debt. When he looked at the signature on the check, he recognized the name of the cattleman from Fort Worth. Turning to Dr. Ironside, he said, "Harry, God sold the cattle."

"Harry, God sold the cattle."

Are you also dreaming dreams and seeing visions? Is the Spirit of God moving in your life with concern to reach the thousands of people who couldn't care less about Jesus Christ? Let me introduce you to the God Elijah knew with intimacy, the God who said, "Go hide yourself," and who also said, "I'll feed you. I'll give you drink."

Next we come to two verses which, I must confess, my heart leaps to because they are so in contrast to my own experience. Verses 5 and 6 tell of the response of this man of God. There was the command and the promise. But there must be a response. "So he did what the LORD had told him. He went to the Kerith Ravine, east of the Jordan, and stayed there. The ravens brought him bread and meat in the morning and bread and meat in the evening, and he drank from the brook."

I mentioned earlier that if I had been in Elijah's place, I would have been conducting an argument with God. You know, there is a lot of humor in the Scriptures, and Acts 9 contains one of the most human of the incidents.

As the chapter opens, we are introduced to the early church's public enemy number one—Saul. "Still breathing out murderous threats," he is en route from Jerusalem to Damascus when he meets the risen Christ and is revolutionized. "When he came to Jerusalem, he tried to join the disciples, but they were all afraid of him, not believing that he really was a disciple" (9:26). I think I overhear one of them saying, "Look, how sharp can you get? This man feigns conversion in order to get on the inside of the group and find out who are identified with the group, and then he'll proceed to liquidate us one by one. Oh, no. We're not taking him in."

It is hard for me to relate this to contemporary Christianity. We open the doors of the church and the people come forward and we ask them profound questions, such as, "You know Jesus Christ as your Savior, don't you?" If they have half a brain cell functioning, they know how to answer. So when I read a section like this, I find it difficult to relate to.

Beginning at verse 10 of the same chapter, we get a flash of insight as to why the disciples were skeptical of Saul's conversion:

> In Damascus there was a disciple named Ananias. The Lord called to him in a vision, "Ananias!"
> "Yes, Lord," he answered.
> The Lord told him, "Go ["Yes, sir"] to the house of Judas on Straight Street ["Roger"] and ask for a man from Tarsus named Saul ["Got it"]."

I don't think Ananias heard a word from here on out. How do I know? He prayed, and in his prayer he proceeded to give God a little information. Did you ever do that in your praying? Look at verse 13: " 'Lord . . . I have heard many reports about this man and all the harm he has done to your saints [and I'm one of them] in Jerusalem. And he has come here with authority from the chief priests to arrest all who call on your name.' "

Now I know you have a period in your text, but I do not believe there should be a period here. I don't think Ananias ever finished his prayer. God interrupted: "Go!" When God first told Ananias to go, Ananias argued, "Lord, are you apprised of all the facts?" But now he stopped debating. And he went and put his hands on Saul (v. 17) and called him Brother Saul. How would you like his assignment? How would you like to put your hands on public enemy number one, recently converted? You would not be sure but what this man might get up from his knees and put air between your head and your body.

When God told Elijah (who had been so successful in the dramatic ministry in the palace), "Go hide yourself," there was not a word of debate or argument. "He did what the LORD had told him." The opposite of ignorance in the spiritual realm is not knowledge, it is obedience.

"The opposite of ignorance in the spiritual realm is not knowledge, it is obedience."

> "To obey is better than sacrifice,
> and to heed is better than the fat of rams"
> (1 Samuel 15:22).

The Lord and I have a running argument. I constantly attempt to impress him with how much I know. He constantly seeks to impress me with how little I have obeyed.

Now turn to the test: "Some time later the brook dried up because there had been no rain in the land" (1 Kings 17:7). What a revolting development!

"Lord, didn't you tell me to come here?"

"Right."

"How can I be in the center of your will and have a dried up brook?"

My friends, God is not simply interested in the impartation of your faith; he is interested in the *development* of your faith. And he knows that faith only develops under pressure, it only develops in the crucible.

God called Abraham out of Ur of the Chaldees, across the Fertile Crescent, and down into the land. He no sooner arrived in the center of the will of God, the place of plenty, than there was a severe famine. The first thing he did was head for Egypt, and what a pack of trouble he got into.

I see some thrilling testimonies of the leadership of the Lord in the life of our seminary students. Here is a young college man, extremely gifted, well-trained, who graduates and goes into a professional field where he is eminently successful. Every time he turns around he receives another advancement. But spiritually he is fed up. "This isn't it. There's no fulfillment here for me." He feels the call of God upon his life, and he resigns his position and sells his house. God has called him to train for vocational Christian work and he lands in Dallas. At the end of the third week of his first semester he surveys the scene. He still has no job. He is beginning to think he is highly qualified to be utterly useless. His wife is sick. And furthermore, he gets three exams returned through the mailbox, each one marked with an "F." He doesn't know much Greek yet, but he knows enough English to realize that the "F" does not stand for "fine."

I have seen such a student with these exams clutched in his hand. He stands in my office and says, "Prof, what happened? I have never been more convinced that I am directly in the will of God. But I have no job, my wife is sick, and I'm flunking three courses." I have often said, "My friend, this is as much a part of the curriculum God has designed to shape you as the courses in which you are enrolled."

Our Lord illustrates this principle in Mark 4. In this chapter you have a portion of our Savior's teacher-training program as he attempted to groom a handful of men for a ministry of multiplication. He presented a series of parables that focused on the subject of faith, but he knew that we do not learn faith by lecture, we learn faith in the laboratory of life. Our Lord was a good teacher. He gave examinations, but not of the kind we give at the seminary. We give cramming exams, where we test to see how much the student can cram in his head.

"That day [the day they had just heard the lectures on faith from the world's greatest teacher] when evening came, he [the Lord] said to his disciples, 'Let us go over to the other side' " (v. 35). So they took off across the water. "A furious squall came up, and the waves broke over the boat, so that it was nearly swamped" (v. 37). That is his way of telling us they had had it. This was a hopeless case. This was a group of professiona fishermen who had spent all their lives on that lake, and they had never seen such a storm. So they came to the Lord, who interestingly enough was asleep in the back of the boat. To translate it graphically, they said, "Lord, don't you even care that we're going down?" The implication is, "At least you can help us bail out." Then the Lord rebuked the wind and the waves, and there was no problem. The wind ceased; there was a great calm.

Then the Lord said to them, "Why are you so afraid? Do you still have no faith?" (v. 40). The little word *you* is in the emphatic position. "How is it that you, of all people, have no faith, you who just heard the lecture?" They wrote an exam, and it came back with a big "F" on it, which was not for "faith."

I have asked myself, Suppose Jesus Christ were to return to speak personally to my own, or your own, church congregation. What would he say? Is it possible that with all the graciousness and compassion of his heart, he would turn to us as an audience and say, "How is it that you, of all people, have no faith?" Privilege creates responsibility. Revelation demands response. God has commanded. He has promised. The next step is ours. It is a step of obedience. But mark it well. The moment we take a significant step of obedience, we're going to be put into the crucible, we're going to be tested. We're going to have to write an exam on our faith.

I am sure many people—perhaps you—are sitting today by a drying brook. It could be financial. It could be physical. It could be intellectual, for those in school. It could be emotional. It could be spiritual. And you're asking, "Lord, what happened?" And he answers, "Nothing. I'm just answering your prayer."

Put yourself in Elijah's position for just a moment. Here he sits and the brook diminishes. It becomes a trickle; then only a few puddles are left; then even they evaporate. How do you respond to that? I have the highest respect for Elijah. I wouldn't have been able to sit there and

"The moment we take a significant step of obedience, we're going to be put into the crucible, we're going to be tested."

watch the brook diminish. I would have gotten out my road map and been looking for every water hole in the area. My motto would have been: "Don't just sit there. Do something." But Elijah sat by the drying brook, and can you imagine what he must have thought? "How come the brook is drying up? What caused that?" Finally it dawned on him with impact—the brook is drying up because he prayed that it would. "He [Elijah] prayed earnestly that it would not rain, and it did not rain on the land for three and a half years" (James 5:17).

Sometimes we have asked, "Lord, make me like your Son." And he took us at our word and began the process and we said, "Lord, what happened? Why did you allow this to come into my life? What are you doing with this drying brook?" He answers, "Nothing, except answering your prayer." For never forget, Jesus Christ, "although he was a son, he learned obedience from what he suffered" (Hebrews 5:8).

Perhaps the Spirit of God is saying to many of us today, "I want to minister through you. But before I can ever minister *through* you, I must minister *to* you." Don't despise the educational experience of your drying brook. Don't throw in the towel. Don't perform an abortion upon the divinely devised process. Let patience have her perfect work, that you may be mature and complete. He wants to make you just like his Son.

THE CONFLICT

God's methods invariably involve a man. But what kind of man does God choose and use? God's choice of material is diametrically opposed to man's. Man chooses an individual on the basis of what he is. God chooses an individual on the basis of what he is to become. When we last saw Elijah, he was sitting by a drying brook, in the process of becoming. God was ministering *to* him. Now He is prepared to minister *through* him.

I suppose there is no more dramatic scene in all Scripture than the contest on Mount Carmel. I wish I were an artist and could render the scene. Two explosive personalities collide, and the moment they do, the sparks fly. Ahab says to Elijah, "Is that you, you troubler of Israel?" (1 Kings 18:17). Elijah is equal to the occasion. Like Nathan the prophet, he points his finger and says, "You are the man." He scores Ahab for his sin and in so doing throws down the gauntlet. There is no question in my mind who is in charge here. Seven times over Elijah takes the initiative. He issues the commands. He issues the initial command—the battle of the gods.

This was a national holiday in Israel. I can see them now, streaming up to the top of that mountain with its commanding view of the Mediterranean Sea. They are coming up by every available route to witness the battle of the gods, fifteen

"Elijah is concerned that the people do not emerge from this contest firmly planted in midair."

rounds, winner take all. And it is a scene of contrasts. By far the overwhelming majority are gathered on the side of the 850 prophets of Baal and the prophets of the grove, clad in their expensive, beautifully colored garments. Around each neck hangs a piece of metal deliberately designed to catch and reflect the rays of the sun, for they worshiped the sun. Soon that group parts for the grand entry of the king. He is borne on a litter by his retinue of servants. He is resplendently robed as well, with all his regal garments. Then your eye shifts. On the other side is a lone, gaunt man, crudely clothed, coarse in appearance, hair disheveled, eyes like steel. Someone says, "Isn't it a shame? He's so lonely." My friends, don't feel sorry for Elijah, because Elijah does not feel sorry for himself.

Mark in your Bible, or at least underline in your mind, the seven statements of Elijah which unfold the story. It's a familiar story, but through this route we can derive the practical lessons which emerge.

Elijah begins by preaching a clear, concise sermon: "How long will you waver between two opinions?" (18:21). He scores the people with the sin of indecisiveness. They are at the fork. He says, "You're going to have to make a decision." Elijah would have had no sympathy with the politician who, when asked, "Are you for or against this issue?" replied, "Well, some of my friends are for it. Some of my friends are against it. And I'm for my friends." Elijah is concerned that the people do not emerge from this contest firmly planted in midair. He tells them, "You're going to have to make a choice. You've been straddling the fence, but there is no room for peaceful coexistence. It's either Jehovah or Baal. Make your choice." And in so saying, he stuns them into absolute silence.

He speaks again, underscoring the problem: "I am the only one of the LORD's prophets left." And then he makes a proposal: "You call on the name of your god, and I will call on the name of the LORD. The god who answers by fire—he is God" (v. 24). Baal was the chief deity in the

Canaanite pantheon. He was the lord of heaven. Whenever it would thunder, whenever they would see lightning flash across the sky, they would exclaim, "That's Baal. That's Baal." He was the lord of fire. If there is anything a god of fire ought to be able to do, it's light a fire. So the people answer, "What you say is good. That's an equitable arrangement. In fact, it's decidedly to our advantage. We agree."

The third statement is found in verse 25: "You go first," Elijah tells them. "Choose one of the bulls and prepare it first. . . . Call on the name of your god, but do not light the fire." This they do, and all morning they perform their weird dancing around the altar and chant monotonously, "O Baal, answer us."

"But there was no response; no one answered"—because, my Bible tells me, false gods have eyes, but they see not; they have ears, but they hear not; they have mouths, but they speak not; they have hands and feet, but they do not move in response to those who call upon them (Psalm 115:2-8). There is dreadful silence. And the priests of Baal leap upon the altar.

Then when the sun is at its hottest, when the god they worship is at his zenith, Elijah, his tongue laden with sarcasm, inserts the needle. He had a fantastic sense of humor. This must have been the most enjoyable part of the experience.

"At noon Elijah began to taunt them. 'Shout louder!' he said. 'Surely he is a god!' " (v. 27). How ridiculous can you get? If he is a god, he certainly can hear. But cry a little louder. Maybe the batteries in his hearing aid are dead. Maybe he's deep in thought. So don't interrupt him. Or maybe he's busy collecting something to eat. Or maybe he's on a journey. He's taking a little vacation in Florida. Maybe he's asleep. He had an overdose of Sominex last night and he has to be awakened. These words stir the people into a frenzy: "So they shouted louder and slashed themselves with swords and spears, as was their custom, until their blood flowed" (v. 28).

Mark this, my friends: If it is sincerity that

"If it is sincerity that saves, these people would have been saved. They were the most sincere people in all the world, but they were sincerely wrong."

saves, these people would have been saved. They were the most sincere people in all the world, but they were sincerely wrong. They had the wrong object for their faith, and faith is always determined by its object.

Suppose I were to wander around in Chicago looking for some unsuspecting individual and I find a guy and I ask, "Say, friend. Would you fly me to Dallas?"

"Dallas," he asks. "Where's that?"

"Well, it's south and a little west of here."

"Sure, I'll be glad to fly you."

So we go out to what is supposed to be a plane. The fuselage is held together by baling wire. It has half a prop, and the tail assembly is missing. And I ask him, "By the way, you have been up before, haven't you?"

"No, as a matter of fact, I've never been up before, but I'm fascinated by flying. Hop in."

If I would get into that plane with that pilot, it would not be faith, it would be foolishness. Because the object of my faith would be worthless. "There was no response, no one answered, no one paid attention" (v. 29).

In his fourth statement, Elijah invites the people, "Come here to me" (v. 30). That is, "Move in a little closer. I don't want you to think there is any chicanery to my method of procedure. I want you to witness the whole thing." Then he proceeds to repair the altar which had been broken down and to dig a trench.

Then in verse 33 is the fifth statement. He commands, "Fill four large jars with water and pour it on the offering and on the wood." I heard an individual of the liberal persuasion reciting this story, and he stopped at this juncture and said, "Now here is another clear-cut evidence of the inconsistency of the Scripture. They were in the midst of a prolonged drought. There was not enough water to feed the cattle. Men were dying for lack of moisture. And Elijah commands them to fill four barrels of water. Now where would they find that?" And I thought, *This man has forgotten his geography.* Mount Carmel is located beside the Mediterranean Sea. Salt water is bad news for cattle and for men, but it is exquisitely designed for dousing wood.

I think Elijah enjoyed this. "Say, men, run down there to the sea and fill up four barrels," he tells them. Down they go and back they come. They douse the altar. He looks at it. "I really don't think it's wet enough, men. Try it again." So down they go the second time and they come back and saturate it. "It's better, but it's still not good enough. You don't mind making another trip down there, do you?" So down they go again. They come back and everything is one soggy mess. Water has even filled up the trench. It is as if Elijah's faith is so great that he would even put obstacles in the way of God.

In verse 36 is his sixth statement. He prayed: "O LORD, God of Abraham, Isaac, and Israel. . . ." Note the content of his prayer: "Let it be known today that you are God in Israel and that I am your servant and have done all these things at your command." That sounds like his words to Ahab in 17:1. He prays that these people, like himself, might be convinced of the reality of Jehovah and might realize that Elijah is merely his representative.

"I have not found stones to be good kindling; but on Mount Carmel they were consumed as well as the dust."

This prayer is quite a contrast to the prayers of the false prophets that lasted more than six hours. " 'Answer me, O LORD, answer me, so these people will know that you, O LORD, are God, and that you are turning their hearts back again.' Then the fire of the LORD fell and burned up the sacrifice [no problem here], the wood [ideal kindling], the stones, and the soil . . ." (18:37-38). You know, I've been camping a great deal and I have not found stones to be good kindling; but on Mount Carmel they were consumed as well as the dust. When I want to put a fire out, I use a pail of dust. And it "licked up [evaporated] the water in the trench." Seeing this, the people "fell prostrate and cried, 'The LORD—he is God! The LORD—he is God!' " (v. 39).

In the morning Baal-worship had prevailed. At the end of this day Jehovah-worship was back in the ascendancy.

The last word, the seventh (found in verse 40) is a drastic word, the sentence of judgment. " 'Seize the prophets of Baal. Don't let anyone get away!' They seized them, and Elijah had them brought down to the Kishon Valley and slaughtered there." You say, That's extreme, isn't it? I think not. Remember there was a malignancy in the nation, and this had to be thoroughly excised before there would be any lasting value. Elijah, a spiritual surgeon, knew he had to hurt in order to heal. I think many times we look back with our perverted perspective and sit in judgment without taking into account the effect of sin not judged with severity.

I want to underscore for your thinking three principles that spring from this portion of the Word of God, principles that answer the question, What kind of man does God choose and use?

In the first place, I believe *God uses one who is convinced that one plus God constitutes a distinct majority.* Divine mathematics are vastly different from human mathematics. We are impressed by numbers; God is not. We are enamored with addition; God is committed to multiplication. Eight hundred and fifty to one? That's not the equation. It is 850 to one *plus God.* And the significance is not the one, but the God who controls the one.

I love to study the gospels to see how God launched the church. It's conceivable to me that an infinite God could have used an infinite number of means. But why did he launch the church the way he did? I believe it was because this was to become a pattern for our ministry.

When you read the gospels, it's obvious that our Lord's paramount ministry was not to the multitudes (who for the most part followed him for superficial reasons) but to a small band of men, into whose lives he built quality and spiritual impact.

In the book of Acts we read that the pagan world testified that these men had "turned the world upside down" (17:6 KJV). At the end of Acts we discover that the church, starting with a handful of men, was closer to reaching its world for Christ than we are after these many hundreds of years, with all the methods, with all the technological advances at our disposal. In the spiritual realm, it is never how many, it is always what kind. The question is not, What can we do? The question is, What can God do? "But we're so few." We're overwhelmed by the size of our group rather than by the size of our God. The size of my God will determine the size of everything in my theology and everything in my Christian experience.

One of my favorite pastimes is watching surgery. I have a friend who specializes in microscopic surgery of the middle ear. Some time ago he said, "I want you to see an operation the likes of which you have never seen. It's the most dramatic operation I have performed." They have perfected an operation today in which they keep the patient under partial anesthesia in order to determine the success of the operation. During the surgery the surgeon was looking through one microscope and I was looking through the other. He pointed out two small bones to me. "They are separated and this is the reason this man has not heard for twenty-six years. Now," he said, "I'm going to join these bones and I'm going to continue to speak. And I want you to keep your eyes on his face. If the operation is successful, you'll know it immediately." So I waited with expectancy and sheer excitement. Finally he said, "I'm coming to it now," and he joined the two bones and continued to talk. I watched the man's face. His eyes became like saucers. "What's that? Who's talking?" he said, and tears began to stream down his face. A man who had not heard for twenty-six years was able to hear again.

If you and I were going through the human body, examining the component parts, and came upon these two bones—if we could see them—we'd say in our lack of expertise, "Who needs these? They're so small." But size does not determine significance. If you can hear today, it is because those two little bones in your ear, which

"The question is not, What can we do? The question is, What can God do?"

"Problems are circumstances to which faith has often capitulated."

you probably were never aware of, are properly joined. The problem with most of us is that we are not properly joined to the infinite God. But any believer in proper relationship with him constitutes a distinct majority, in any situation, in any age.

I want you to notice a second principle here: *God uses a man,* as he did Elijah, *who is not problem-oriented but who is potential-oriented.* I'm sure Elijah could have wrung his hands and said, "Things are rough. Seven thousand—but they're in a cave. And I'm on Carmel. What can I do?"

Wherever I go, I am interested to see how an individual will tip his hand in the first moments of conversation with me. I spend a lot of time with pastors and Christian workers. Sometimes they pick me up at the airport. I get into the car and right away they start telling me about their problems. When I ask Christians, "How are you doing?" many answer, "Oh, pretty well—under the circumstances." That is where they spend the bulk of their lives—under the circumstances! Problems are circumstances to which faith has often capitulated.

I ran across an interesting statement in my reading the other day: "We are all faced with a series of great opportunities, brilliantly disguised as unsolvable problems." A church that has no problems is probably paralyzed. If you're making progress for God, you have problems. The question is, Where are your eyes?

Numbers 13 records that the children of Israel, wending their way through the wilderness, came to a place called Kadesh Barnea, actually just a wide spot in the road. Here they made a decision that determined their destiny. God told them to go directly into the land, but they said, "Let's not play the part of a fool. Let's be practical. Let's appoint a committee." So in typical committee fashion, they came back with a majority and a minority report. Verse 30 gives the minority report: "Then Caleb silenced the people before Moses and said, 'We should go up and take possession of the land, for we can certainly do it.' " He believed they were well-able because he believed God was well-able. But then the majority gave their report:

> But the men who had gone up with him said, "We can't attack those people; they are stronger than we are." And they spread among the Israelites a bad report about the land they had explored. They said, "The land we explored devours those living in it. All the people we saw there are of great size. We saw the Nephilim there (the descendants of Anak come from the Nephilim). We seemed like grasshoppers in our own eyes, and we looked the same to them" (vv. 31-33).

Probably every child enrolled in your Sunday school can give you the names of the two men who brought the minority report. I defy you to give the name of even one of the ten men who brought the majority report. They are all found in the opening of chapter 13, but who wants to remember them? In America we often say, "The majority is always right." Really? The majority is frequently flat wrong.

What was the difference between these two groups? I believe the majority was problem-oriented. "They're giants—redwood variety, Texas-size. Besides, we're just a bunch of God's grasshoppers." What was the difference in Joshua and Caleb? They had seen the giants too. And I don't think they had an inordinate view of themselves. They would have agreed, "We're just a group of God's grasshoppers." The only difference was that they saw more. They saw God.

When you read through the life of our Savior, you come to the statement, "He did not do many miracles there [in Nazareth] because of their lack of faith" (Matthew 13:58). The difficulty of the problem was not hindrance; it was the refusal of the people to believe that he was who he claimed to be—the Son of God. With us, I believe "faith" is often figuring what God can do without embarrassment and then asking him to do it. But we do not put him in a bind. We are afraid to ask him

> "God uses a man
> who does not
> focus his attention
> on his ability but
> rather on his
> availability."

to do the impossible, because there are so many problems.

A third principle, I believe, is that *God uses a man who does not focus his attention on his ability but rather on his availability.* But you say, "I don't have much." My friend, you have all that God intended you to have. "But I can't do much." You can do all that God wants you to do. If you continue to focus on your ability or lack of it, God will never use you. "Now it is required that those who have been given a trust must prove faithful" (1 Corinthians 4:2). Not brilliant, not gifted, not spectacular—faithful. The longer I study the life of Elijah, the more I am convinced that what James said of him is true. He was a man just like us (James 5:17). He was an ordinary man who lived an extraordinary life. That is his greatest claim to distinction.

Have you ever wondered what goes through the mind of a professor before a class begins? I'll tell you. I have often sat there at my desk and looked at a student and thought, *Lord, what are you going to do with him? How will he ever make it?* I remember one student I had a number of years ago. He slept through most of my classes. He might as well have slept through all of them. How he graduated, I'll never know.

After graduation he pastored a church up in Canada. The church was 123 years old, and at the end of 123 years of existence it was smaller than when it was first organized. Nineteen pastors in a row had walked away from it as a hopeless situation. And he took the pastorate. I thought, *Well, that's par for the course. He doesn't know enough not to take it.* He moved into the church, but what was more important, God moved into his life. And dramatic, divinely supernatural things began to happen. Wherever I went, I would hear about this man and his work. One day he wrote me a letter and said, "I understand you're coming up to our area. I'm going to be gone for a little vacation. I'd love to have you preach to my people." I wrote back and said, "I'd love to preach for you. I'd like to see this thing firsthand."

When I arrived at the church, the first thing I noticed was they had begun a building program for expansion—the first new building in 123 years. The sanctuary was so crowded that when I got up to preach, I gave my seat to a man who had been standing. After the service one of the deacons came up and said, "Well, that's pretty good preaching, son." Then he added, "By the way, have you ever heard our preacher preach?" I didn't dare tell him I taught their preacher homiletics.

I went back to the seminary with a new lease on life. What am I doing? Erecting a monument to mediocrity? Absolutely not. But I have been at the seminary long enough to learn that brilliance is sterile unless it is coupled with commitment. Does God use a dull tool rather than a sharp one? I do not think so, except that oftentimes the sharp one is not available.

I want to say something that I believe needs to be said. You may say, "My, it must be wonderful to be able to preach, to be able to teach in a seminary and multiply yourself." It is. But I only preach and I only teach for one reason: God has gifted me to do it, and I would prostitute the gifts were I not to use them. I never chose these gifts. Nobody ever told me to go to a Christian "gift shop" and pick this one, this one, and this one. God sovereignly bestowed these gifts upon me and upon those who are serving him. And he sovereignly bestowed you with a gift. Don't despise the gift. Your problem is not your ability. Your problem is your availability. When we get to heaven, there are some people who are going to compel some of us who have sustained a dramatic, public ministry to step down lower while they move up higher, because it is required of a steward, not that he be brilliant, not that he sustain a public ministry, but that he be faithful in the ministry to which God has called him.

". . . brilliance is sterile unless it is coupled with commitment."

COMMUNICATION FROM GOD

*I*f you were asked to choose a pattern for your prayer life, it is unlikely you would select Elijah. "After all," you might quite reasonably argue, "Elijah was a mighty prophet of God, and I am not. Elijah was a mighty worker of miracles, and I certainly am not." Somehow we have managed to wrap Elijah in a mantle of supernaturalism, with the result that he is unapproachable. He's in another league. But it is not thus that the New Testament remembers him. James 5:17-18 is a highly instructive and illuminating passage of Scripture.

Let me remind you of two things concerning James. In the first place, the epistle of James has more to say about the doctrine of prayer than any other New Testament epistle. The book is drenched with this doctrine. Second, James was nicknamed "Camel knees" by the early church, so calloused were his knees from incessant praying. When the Holy Spirit wants to teach us the doctrine of prayer, he selects a practitioner, not a theorist. Doctrine is dynamic. Truth is designed not to satisfy your curiosity but to overhaul your experience. But the question nags: Who was it who motivated "Camel knees"? Who turned him on? Who was his pattern?

James 5:17 provides the answer. Out of all of the possibilities, we read "Elijah was a man just like us. He prayed earnestly. . . ." The Word of

God does not say, "Elijah was a mighty prophet of God, and he prayed." It does not say, "Elijah was a mighty worker of miracles, and he prayed." It says, "Elijah was a man just like us." He was cut from the same bolt of human cloth. He had problems, he had perplexities, he had fears, he had doubts, he had frustrations. But he prayed. That's what made him different. That's why "Camel knees" selects him as his paragon for prayer. I believe the New Testament is saying to us that if Elijah is like us in our passions, we may be like him in our prayer.

With this biblical backdrop, let's return to 1 Kings 18 and see Elijah in communication. We have viewed Elijah in confrontation. We have seen him in concealment beside a drying brook. We have seen him in conflict, in the dramatic action on Carmel. Now we focus our attention on him in communication.

This is certainly not the first time we read of his prayer life. Elijah had prayed that it might not rain. Prayer preceded his encounter with King Ahab. On Mount Carmel, it was prayer that brought down the descending fire. Now, the descending flood.

God had promised that it would rain: "After a long time, in the third year, the word of the LORD came to Elijah: 'Go and present yourself to Ahab, and I will send rain on the land' " (18:1). If God promised to send rain, why pray? Prayer is the hand of faith that translates promise into performance. God not only ordains the end, he also ordains the means. It is not a question of coming to a reluctant God in an attempt to persuade him to do what he really does not want to do; it is a matter of coming to God with a consciousness that we are dependent individuals. Prayer is the realization that our need is not partial, it's total.

Shortly after I became a Christian, someone wrote in the flyleaf of my Bible this couplet:

When I try, I fail.
When I trust, He succeeds.

There is a world of theology in that couplet. The Christian life is not a matter of trying, it is a matter of trusting. It is a recognition that the believing life is not difficult, it's impossible, apart from supernatural invasion.

There are three characteristics of Elijah's prayer life which I trust the Spirit of God will weave into the fabric of our experience. First note *the earnestness of his prayer.*

"And Elijah said to Ahab, 'Go, eat and drink, for there is the sound of a heavy rain.' " (v. 41). (We discover in a subsequent verse that there were no clouds in the sky. How can you hear the sound of a heavy rain when there is not a cloud in the sky? That's the ear of faith. The ear of faith hears when you cannot see.) "So Ahab went off to eat and drink [note the contrast], but Elijah climbed up to the top of Carmel, bent down to the ground and put his face between his knees" (v. 42).

The text mentions the posture, I think, not because this is to be the pattern but because the posture is outward evidence of inward earnestness. You remember our Lord in the Garden of Gethsemane prostrated himself on the ground when he cried, "If it is possible, may this cup be taken from me. Yet not as I will, but as you will" (Matthew 26:39). His position was a reflection of the attitude of his heart.

James says, "He prayed earnestly." This can be quite literally translated, "He prayed in his prayer." That's a good thought. Very few of us do that.

Isn't it refreshing to listen to a new convert pray? Not long ago we led a man to Christ through our home Bible class ministry. He came to know the Lord on Thursday evening, and in the follow-up session that night we said, "The purpose of this class has been fulfilled in your life. It's designed to lead you to the Savior. We would encourage you now to come to our church, where you can build on this foundation." So he showed up Sunday morning. The pastor announced that we would have an evening service. This man didn't know enough to stay home, so he showed up again. In the evening, the pastor announced that we would have

". . . the believing life is not difficult, it's impossible, apart from supernatural invasion."

Bible study and prayer meeting on Wednesday. Again not knowing enough not to come, he showed up.

Before the prayer session, he turned to me and asked, "Do you think they'd mind if I prayed?"

"Of course not," I said. "That's what we're here for."

"I know, but I've got a problem. I can't pray the way you people do."

I said, "Friend, that's no problem. Thank God for that."

But, you know, after a while, he'll learn the clichés and the jargon and he'll be saying his prayers like the rest of us.

A number prayed, and finally I put my hand over on his thigh to encourage him. And I'll never forget his prayer. He said, "Lord, this is Jim. I'm the one that met you last Thursday night. Forgive me, Lord, because I can't say it the way the rest of these people do, but I want to tell you the best I know how. I love you, Lord. Amen." And he ignited the prayer meeting. We had been doing a fantastic job scraping the Milky Way. But he prayed.

Someday I'm going to write a book on the things my children have taught me about theology. A good many years ago, a scholar was visiting my home. He happened to come during meal and family worship time, so I invited him to join us. My children were quite small then, and in typical childlike fashion, they thanked Jesus for the tricycle and the sandbox and the fence. I could tell that our visitor could scarcely wait to get me into the living room.

"Professor Hendricks, you don't mean to tell me that you teach in a theological seminary and yet you teach your children to pray for things like that?"

"I certainly do. Do you ever pray about your Ford?" I knew he did; he was riding mostly on faith and fabric.

"I certainly do."

"Well, what made you think your Ford is more important to God than my boy's tricycle?" I pressed him further. "Do you ever pray for protection?"

"Brother Hendricks, I never go on the highways but what I pray for protection."

"That's what my boy is thanking Jesus for when he thanks him for the fence. That fence keeps out those great big dogs on the other side!"

Do you know what our problem is? Most of us are educated beyond our intelligence. It's refreshing to have a new convert move into our midst, or a child who in simplicity and earnestness of heart cries out to God. God delights to react to the earnestness of a believing heart.

Now notice the second characteristic of Elijah's prayer life—*the expectation of his prayer*. If you underline three statements in three verses, you'll see the story of an answer to prayer. In verse 43, underline the statement "There is nothing there"; in verse 44, "A cloud as small as a man's hand is rising"; in verse 45, "A heavy rain came on." Nothing, a small cloud, and a heavy rain. And the key? Elijah prayed expectantly.

> "Go and look toward the sea," he told his servant. And he went up and looked.
> "There is nothing there," he said.
> Seven times Elijah said, "Go back."
> The seventh time the servant reported, "A cloud as small as a man's hand is rising from the sea."
> So Elijah said, "Go and tell Ahab, 'Hitch up your chariot and go down before the rain stops you' " (vv. 43-44).

My friend, most of us would have thrown in the towel a long time before this. Suppose Elijah had stopped on the sixth time? But in expectant faith, he sends the servant out to scan the skies because he is looking for something. If we expect nothing, we will seldom be disappointed.

I mentioned before that there is a great deal of humor in the Bible. Acts 12 is another choice case in point. Verse 5: "So Peter was kept in prison, but the church was earnestly praying to God for him." God answers their prayer. "When this had dawned on him [Peter], he went to the house of Mary the mother of John, also called Mark,

"It's refreshing to have a new convert move into our midst, or a child who in simplicity and earnestness of heart cries out to God."

"But fortunately the answer to their prayer kept knocking. And if I know Peter, about this time he would have been knocking awfully hard."

where many people had gathered and were praying" (v. 12). For what were they praying? Peter's deliverance. "Peter knocked at the outer entrance, and a servant girl named Rhoda came to answer the door. When she recognized Peter's voice, she was so overjoyed she ran back without opening it and exclaimed, 'Peter is at the door' " (vv. 13-14).

Do you get the picture? This little girl looks out through the hatch: "Good night! It's Peter." She's so excited, she forgets to open the door. She runs back. "Hey, Peter's out there." And did they stand to sing the "Hallelujah Chorus" or "Praise God from Whom All Blessings Flow"? No, they said to her, "You're out of your mind." But she insisted that it was so.

Can't you visualize the scene as this dear girl says, "Look, I saw him." "No, not Peter. You're seeing things." She would not be put down with that. So they came up with a more profound theological answer: "Oh, well, then it's his angel." They weren't praying for his angel to be delivered. But fortunately the answer to their prayer kept knocking. And if I know Peter, about this time he would have been knocking awfully hard. When they finally opened the door and saw him, "they were astonished" (v. 16). That's the mildest translation I can think of. A more literal translation would be: "They were dumbfounded—knocked out."

Now before you crawl all over them, suppose somebody came up to you today and said, "You know what you've been praying for for twenty-two years?"

"Yes, sir. It's been the great burden of my heart."

"You have the answer."

"I what?"

"The Lord answered your prayer."

"Don't put me on."

"Really, your loved one received Christ as his Savior."

"No, you must have somebody else in mind. Is his name Bill?"

"Right. He's saved."

"Let me see him. I can't believe it."

Oh, may Elijah's tribe increase. "God said it will rain. In fact, I can hear it. Go look for it."

"Nothing."

"Go look again."

"Nothing."

"It's coming. Look."

And it came.

"Daddy, do you think Jesus would mind if I asked him for a shirt?"

My wife and I began a procedure I would strongly recommend to any parent. When our children came along, my wife and I took a little looseleaf notebook, and on one side of a page we wrote, "We ask" and on the other side, "He answers." I wouldn't trade anything for this little book because of what it enabled me to teach my children about prayer, to teach them different aspects of expectation.

With Elijah, and often with us, there is a clear-cut yes. God said this, that's what he does. What an exciting thing for a child.

We have a lovely family in our community. The father felt God was compelling him into vocational Christian work. So he sold his business at a loss and entered the work to which the Lord had called him. And things got rather rough financially.

One night at family devotions, Timmy, the youngest of four boys, asked, "Daddy, do you think Jesus would mind if I asked him for a shirt?"

"Of course not," answered his dad.

So they wrote in their little prayer-request book, "Shirt for Timmy." Mom added, "Size seven." You can be sure that every night Timmy saw to it that they prayed for the shirt. For weeks they prayed for it—every night.

One day the mother received a telephone call from a Christian businessman, a clothier in downtown Dallas. He said, "I just completed our July clearance sale. Knowing that you have four boys it occurred to me that I have something you might use. Could you use some boys' shirts?"

She said, "What size?"

"Size seven."

"How many do you have?"

"I have twelve of them."

What would you do? Some parents would take the shirts and stuff them in the bureau drawer and make some casual comment to the child. Not this enlightened family. That night, as expected—"Don't forget, Mommy, let's pray for the shirt."

"We don't have to pray for the shirt, Timmy. The Lord answered your prayer."

"He did?"

"Right."

As previously arranged, brother Tommy goes out, gets the shirt, brings it in, and puts it on the table. Timmy's eyes are like saucers. Tommy goes out, and gets another shirt and brings it in. Out, back, out, back, until he has piled twelve shirts on the table, and Timmy thinks God has gone into the shirt business. There's a boy today by the name of Timmy who still believes that there is a God in heaven who is interested enough in a boy's needs to provide a shirt. Do your kids know that? Do you know that in our affluent society?

Sometimes we have had to write "No" in the answer column. Have you come to appreciate with expectation the Lord's no? This is just as much an answer as a yes. My wife and I prayed for two additional children and God appeared to answer that prayer until the time of their birth. They were both born dead. I can still remember coming home and finding my four kids at the door calling, "Hey, Dad! What is it, a boy or a girl?" And I took them over to our divan and got out our little book and wrote "No" in it.

You will communicate more in one experience like this than in twenty dozen sermons on the subject of prayer. You are coming through at a level the child can understand. The problem often is whether we adults get the message.

Sometimes our expectancy is demonstrated by waiting. Some things on our prayer list were there a long time before they were answered. One of them was the salvation of my father, a retired military officer. Shortly before his retirement, he flew down to Dallas to see us, and of course my kids were so excited. "Granddaddy's coming! Hope he'll wear his uniform."

When he appeared in the doorway of the plane in his uniform with all the varicolored ribbons, my youngest boy took off to greet him. When my father got to the bottom of the ramp, he threw his arms around him. Just as I caught up with them, I overheard my youngest say, "Hey, Granddaddy. Do you know Jesus yet?"

My father said, "No, son, I'm afraid I can't say I do."

"Well, you will pretty soon, cause we're praying for you!" "Pretty soon" turned into many years. Dad received Christ four months prior to his death in 1974. I had personally prayed for him for 42 years.

Have you been praying for many years, perhaps for the salvation of a loved one? May I encourage you on the authority of the Word of God to go to the brow of the hill again, and look. My Savior said, "Keep on asking, and you will receive. Keep on seeking, and you will find. Keep on knocking, and it will be opened to you." But ask and seek and knock with expectancy.

Now I want you to underscore the third characteristic of Elijah's prayer life—*the effect of his prayer*. "Meanwhile, the sky grew black with clouds, the wind rose, a heavy rain came on . . ." (v. 45). There is a twofold effect described in this passage. There is, first, the effect of his prayer upon the land. This was no light drizzle. This was no soft summer shower, enough to moisten the land but not to satisfy the drought. This was a heavy rain that broke the prolonged dry spell. May I say in passing, we are living in spiritually arid conditions. We are surrounded by desert, and God is still looking for a man or woman who is able to bring down the refreshing rain, to break the spiritual drought.

But I also read, in verse 46, that there was a great effect upon this man: "The power of the LORD came upon Elijah and, tucking his cloak into his belt, he ran ahead of Ahab all the way to Jezreel." Elijah himself emerges from the experience with a new dynamic: The power of God was upon him. I cannot think of any greater testimony than this. That's the secret. The power of God was on him because he knew how to lay hold of the throne of God in prayer.

There is a principle here we need to remember: Great praying brings great blessing. Elijah's prayer was great, not because of its language, not because of its length, and certainly not because of its loudness. It was great because it was earnest, it was expectant, and it was invested in the living God.

But it is also a dangerous thing to pray. Elijah had learned that. He had prayed that it would not rain. The answer to his prayer was a drying brook. The disciples learned that. The Lord said, "There's no problem with the harvest; the problem is a shortage of laborers and I want you to pray about it" (*see* Matthew 9:37-38). The interesting thing is that the ones he asked to pray about it were the very men he pressed into service (chapter 10).

When I was a boy I heard Dr. L. L. Legters, a great Bible teacher of the last generation. Frankly, I do not remember very much of what he said, but I have never forgotten an illustration he used. He said that on one occasion when he was pastor of a church, he was walking down the street with fifty dollars in his pocket and he met a missionary home on furlough.

The missionary said, "Dr. Legters, I think it's providential that we met. We're having an urgent prayer meeting at the church. We'd love to have you join us."

Dr. Legters was a somewhat brusque individual, and before they went to prayer, he said, "Now, let's not pray out of ignorance. Let's pray out of intelligence. Exactly what is it that you need?"

"Well," the missionary said, "we have an urgent financial need. We need fifty dollars."

"Fine. Let's pray."

They went all the way around the circle, and when they got through, one of the missionaries said, "I don't feel that we've really laid hold of

the Lord in this. Let's pray some more."
Around they went the second time.

The third time around, Dr. Legters said, God spoke to him: "Legters, what about the fifty dollars in your pocket?" So he stopped a woman right in the middle of her prayer. "Hold it. God answered your prayer."

Dr. Legters put his hand down in his pocket, pulled out the fifty dollars, and put it on the table.

I can still remember his long, bony finger pointing as he said, "Ladies and gentlemen, it's a dangerous thing to pray."

"Don't ever pray unless you want to get involved."

It still is. Don't ever pray unless you want to get involved. Don't ever pray unless you are personally committed, because the answer to your prayer may demand a beginning with you. "You do not have, because you do not ask God. When you ask, you do not receive, because you ask with wrong motives, that you may spend what you get on your pleasures" (James 4:2-3).

I want to ask you a question I have been asking myself for some time now: How do you account for the fact that the one area in your Christian experience in which you are constantly bombed out is your prayer life? My friend, that is not an accident, that's the product of cultivation. The older I become in the faith, the more impressed I am with the subtlety of Satan. He always fogs in the area of the crucial, never the trivial. Satan does not mind your witnessing, as long as you don't pray. Because he knows it is far more important to talk to God about men than to talk to men about God. Satan does not mind your studying the Scriptures, as long as you don't pray, for then the Word will never get into your life. Then you will simply develop a severe case of spiritual pride, and he loves that. Satan doesn't mind your becoming compulsively active in your local church or in some other form of Christian work, just so you do not pray. For then you will be active, but you will not accomplish anything.

The gospels record only fifty-two days in the life of our Lord. Mark 1 tells of one of the busiest recorded days in his life. It was a day crowded

"The work of God today in many areas is languishing, not for lack of divine power but for lack of human prayer."

with the performance of miracles, with teaching, with healing. Only a person who has sustained a public ministry has any idea of the physical and emotional drain of constant interaction with people.

Now notice what our Lord does: "Very early in the morning [the morning after the busiest recorded day in the life of our Lord], while it was still dark, Jesus got up, left the house and went off to a solitary place, where he prayed" (Mark 1:35). If Jesus Christ, who had unbroken fellowship and communion with the Father, needed to pray, what must my need be? What must your need be? But so high on his priority list was intercourse with the infinite God that after a busy day of service, he got up long before sunrise and went to a solitary place to pray.

The work of God today in many areas is languishing, not for lack of divine power but for lack of human prayer. We fight, we war, we bicker, we complain, we scheme, we do everything in the world, James says, but we have not because we ask not.

COMMITMENT AFTER FAILURE

While waiting for my father in his office at the Pentagon some time ago, I picked up a military journal and began to read a fascinating article by Gen. Douglas B. MacArthur, entitled "Requisites for Military Success." He stated four such requisites.

First, there must be *morale*, a will to win. There must be an esprit de corps. There must be a cause worth dying for. Second, there must be *strength*. An army must have adequately trained and well-equipped personnel. Third, there must be an *adequate source of supply*. Life lines must be kept open.

The bulk of the article was devoted to the fourth: In order to win, an army must have a *knowledge of the enemy*. General MacArthur said, "The greater the knowledge of the enemy, the greater the potential of victory." He traced this principle through military history, beginning with General Joshua and ending with the North African campaign in the Second World War where Rommel was finally defeated because of the successful work of counterespionage.

This principle has its parallel in the spiritual realm. Paul knew that, for he told the Corinthians that he did not want Satan to gain an advantage over them (*see* 2 Corinthians 2:11). And then he adds the reason: "For we are not unaware of his schemes." We are not in the dark as

"There is something about victory that elates, that takes you off your guard, that leaves you wide open to the devastating arrows of Satan."

to how the enemy operates. And the greater the knowledge of the enemy, the greater the potential of victory.

In 1 Kings 19, we find a case study in the strategy of Satan. If I were to give a topic sentence to this chapter, I would write across it: "Victory always makes us vulnerable." There is something about victory that elates, that takes you off your guard, that leaves you wide open to the devastating arrows of Satan. In chapter 19 it is a short distance from the top of Carmel to the bottom of the valley of despair.

The thing I appreciate about this record is its realism. It is confirming proof of the inspiration of the Scriptures. When God paints a man, he paints him warts and all. He tells the story as it is. From the standpoint of the narrative, it would have been much nicer, much less threatening, to have ended the story with chapter 18. But this would have been contrary to fact. Paul reminds us, "So, if you think you are standing firm, be careful [stop, look, listen] that you don't fall!" (1 Corinthians 10:12). Where? At the very point we think we're strongest. That's the point at which we are most vulnerable.

Chapters 18 and 19 of 1 Kings are sharply contrasted. The point of Elijah's greatest strength in chapter 18 is the point of his greatest failure in chapter 19. Let's examine this exposé of the devil's devices, for he is still employing the same traps, and he is much more experienced now.

The first trap is *the danger of looking at circumstances* (vv. 1-3).

Ahab came home rather late that night. It had been a long and discouraging day. He hoped that Jezebel had gone to sleep. Perhaps he stepped into the palace silently with his shoes in his hand. Suddenly he heard that all too familiar voice.

"Ahab."

"Yes, dear. I thought you had gone to bed."

"No, I couldn't wait to hear what happened. You look weary."

"Yes, I'm very weary."

"Would you like something to eat?"

"No, thanks. I lost my appetite."

"Well, sit down and have a cup of coffee."

So she served him some Jezebel java.

Then Jezebel began to ask some rather pressing questions. Ahab tried to change the subject.

"Who do you think will win the Samaritan Series?"

"Ahab, you're evading the issue. What happened?"

"Ahab told Jezebel everything Elijah had done and how he had killed all the prophets with the sword. So Jezebel sent a messenger to Elijah to say, 'may the gods deal with me, be it ever so severely, if by this time tomorrow I do not make your life like that of one of them.' Elijah was afraid and ran for his life. When he came to Beersheba in Judah [120 miles south of Jezreel], he left his servant there" (vv. 1-3). Until now, the only thing that had filled Elijah's vision was Jehovah. Now he is looking through the wrong end of the telescope and his perspective is greatly distorted.

This is always true in the spiritual realm. You remember the time Peter and the other disciples were out in a boat. They looked out over the starboard side and saw what, at first, was a horrible sight: "Why it looks as if someone's walking on the water." They were scared to death. But then the Lord spoke and they recognized him. Peter, in his characteristic fashion, said, "Lord, if it's you, tell me to come to you." The Lord said, "Come."

Now Peter has a problem: he has to step over the side of the gunwale and let go. I can see him gingerly taking off across the water, and Philip and Andrew are bug-eyed back in the boat watching him go. Finally Andrew hollers out, "Hey, Peter, watch that wave." And he begins to sink.

Then Peter prays what is in many ways the most significant prayer in the New Testament: "Lord, save me!" (It is also the shortest prayer. If he had prayed like some people do, he would have been twenty feet under.) And the Lord reached down and lifted him out of that watery

"That is the kind of rejoicing I want: rejoicing in the midst of reality."

cavern.

How do you think Peter got back to the boat? I'm quite convinced the Lord didn't carry him back; he walked back. I'm equally confident he kept his eyes on the Lord. The moment you and I begin to take our eyes off the source of our courage, we lose it. The moment you take your eyes off the only adequate one, the only one who can protect you and provide for you, you're going to slip on a spiritual banana peel. You're going to sprawl in the faith.

In the book of Philippians, the apostle Paul says, "Rejoice in the Lord always. I will say it again: Rejoice!" (4:4). I used to read this and think, *My, what wonderful words.* One day I asked myself, "Where did Paul say them?" He didn't say them in the Statler-Hilton, he said them while under house arrest, chained to a Roman guard. We used to sing a song in America years ago—"Oh, what a beautiful morning . . . everything's going my way." Paul sang, "Oh, what a beautiful morning, everything's going in the opposite direction." That is the kind of rejoicing I want: rejoicing in the midst of reality. This is not happiness, which simply depends on happenings, but rejoicing, which depends on reality.

I have often wondered if Elisha learned this lesson from Elijah.

> When the servant of the man of God [Elisha] got up and went out early the next morning, an army with horses and chariots had surrounded the city. "Oh, my lord, what shall we do?" the servant asked.
>
> "Don't be afraid," the prophet answered. "Those who are with us are more than those who are with them."
>
> And Elisha prayed, "O LORD, open his eyes so he may see." Then the LORD opened the servant's eyes, and he looked and saw the hills full of horses and chariots of fire all around Elisha (2 Kings 6:15-17).

Did Elijah teach Elisha the principle demonstrated in this experience: Don't fasten your eyes on circumstances; if you do, you're doomed for a fall. "Greater is he that is in you, than he that is in the world."

I see in verse 4 a second danger to which we are constantly exposed: *the danger of praying foolishly*. Elijah, not satisfied to go 120 miles south, "went a day's journey into the desert. He came to a broom tree, sat down under it and prayed that he might die. 'I have had enough, LORD,' he said. 'Take my life; I am no better than my ancestors.' " Single-handedly he took on 850 prophets, but one woman said, "I'll get you," and he ran. "Lord, I've had it. I'm turning in my prophet's badge."

The longer I examine this, the more I think there is a touch of the hypocritical in Elijah's prayer. Whenever you have distorted perspective, you always become dishonest, even in your praying. I don't think Elijah wanted to die. If he had wanted to die, he did not have to travel 120 miles south. All he had to do was to make himself available to Jezebel. She'd be delighted to accommodate his request.

Have you ever thanked God for the blessings of unanswered prayer? I sometimes think of the moronic things I have asked God for and I'm so glad he never answered them the way I expected.

Prayer is not asking for what *you* want; it is asking for what *he* wants. One of the first verses of Scripture I ever committed to memory was Psalm 37:4:

> "Delight yourself in the LORD
>   and he will give you the desires
>   of your heart."

I can still remember as a young person running that through my mind and saying, "Is that really true? If I delight myself in the Lord, you mean he'll give me anything I want?" That's right. But my problem may have been the same as yours: My occupation was with the desires of my heart, not with the delights of the Lord.

When I was a boy in Philadelphia, I courted a

"Whenever you have distorted perspective, you always become dishonest, even in your praying."

lovely young lady who is now my wife. I lived in northeast Philadelphia and she lived in southwest Philadelphia. We couldn't have been further apart. It took me an hour and three quarters to go from my home to hers. I had to take a trolley car, a bus, a subway train, and another trolley car. I can still remember storming out the front door of my home with my grandmother after me:

"Howard! Come back. You have to do the dishes."

"I'm awfully sorry, Grandma. I don't have time to do the dishes. I've got to see my girl."

And I would get on a trolley car and a bus and a subway train and another trolley car and go all the way across town—to do what? Dishes! But don't feel sorry for me; I cannot even to this day think of anything more delightful than doing dishes in the presence of my wife. Her delights are my desires.

This is exactly what happens in the spiritual realm. His will becomes my will. His way becomes my way. His word becomes my word. And when I am occupied with his delights, then by that strange spiritual metamorphosis, they become my desires. When I come to God in prayer, I pray, "Lord, not what I want, but what you want. Even if it means death at the hands of a Jezebel." Better to die at the hands of a Jezebel in the will of God than to be comfortable and secure in a place outside God's will.

There is a third trap that is becoming higher on my priority list these days because I believe it is higher on the priority list of the enemy. This is *the danger of neglecting physical and emotional needs.* We are living in a pressurized society whose impact you cannot escape. Christians are subject to emotional and to physical problems just like other members of the human family.

Some time ago we had a very gifted student at Dallas who unfortunately lost his perspective in this area. He'd whack away on his sleep so he could study more to prepare himself for the Lord's work. And he got it down to six hours. Then he whittled it to five. When he finally got it to four hours a night, he was elated. He kept telling his wife, who couldn't share the excitement, that he now had to sleep only four hours a night and could spend the rest of the time studying the Word and preparing himself for Christian ministry. It took twenty of us at the seminary to finally get hold of him and get him to professional help.

When his wife went to see the psychiatrist (a man of God who was on our seminary board and taught at a nearby medical school), the first thing he asked was, "Mary, what do you do for relaxation?"

"Well," she said, "we love to fish."

"Wonderful. When's the last time you went fishing?"

She told me later, "Professor Hendricks, it was as if he had pulled back the curtains and suddenly the problem became so transparent."

But I'm afraid it's not so transparent to many Christian workers and many Christian laymen who are overly active, supposedly in the Lord's work. This student tried unsuccessfully to cut down his need for rest and relaxation. He never achieved a constructive ministry.

I got off a plane for a week of meetings in a church pastored by one of our graduates. This man's wife hurriedly took me off to the side while he went to get my bags.

"Professor Hendricks, while you're here, I wonder if you can help my husband. He is constantly active. He spends no time in rest. He is not recouping his strength and his energies, as you often exhorted us to do. I'm afraid he's going to crack up. He's averaging about four to five hours of sleep a night."

A few days went by and we were driving along in the car. I said to him, "How come you don't smoke?"

"How come I don't smoke?"

"Well, I've been here all week and I noticed you haven't lit up once."

"Professor Hendricks, my body is the temple of the Holy Spirit."

"That's wonderful, that's very good thinking. Is that also the reason you're prostituting your

"It's not a question of burning out or rusting out, it's a question of living out."

body with four to five hours of sleep a night?"

It's amazing how spongy our view of the body, the temple of the Holy Spirit, is. We show wisdom in respect to smoking: "My body is the temple of the Holy Spirit. Why put it in the grave prematurely?" By the same logic, why put myself in the grave prematurely by burning the candle at both ends and all along the line?

Elijah was in the valley of despair. And it is in this dismal scene that we are given a beautiful picture of the grace of God. "Then he lay down under the tree and fell asleep. All at once an angel touched him and said, 'Get up and eat.' He looked around, and there by his head was a cake of bread baked over hot coals, and a jar of water. He ate and drank and then lay down again" (1 Kings 19:5-6).

Just think of it—God sent an angel on a mission of mercy to prepare a meal for his servant. The angel awakens him. Elijah eats and, from sheer exhaustion, goes back to sleep again.

"The angel of the LORD came back a second time and touched him and said, 'Get up and eat, for the journey is too much for you' " (v. 7). What journey? A journey out of the will of God. You may be out of God's will, but you are never out of his concern. He graciously, tenderly seeks to throw blocks in your way to prevent certain things and to provide for other basic needs that you have.

"So he got up and ate and drank. Strengthened by that food, he traveled forty days and forty nights until he reached Horeb, the mountain of God" (v. 8). Horeb is more than 200 miles south of Beersheba. So—120 miles plus 200—it is over 320 miles from where Jezebel said, "I'm going to get you," till Elijah finally stops running.

Someone says, "Don't you know it's better to burn out than to rust out?" This is spiritual nonsense, for that's not the option. It's not a question of burning out or rusting out, it's a question of living out. And that takes the balance of the ministry of the Holy Spirit.

I have often told students who come to see me for counsel, "What I think you really need is a good night's sleep." Did you ever wake up in the morning with a severe headache? It's amazing how unspiritual you feel. I have made it a practice never to make a critical decision when I have a headache, or when I am weary. One good night's rest restores perspective. And God gave Elijah the basis for some perspective he wanted Elijah to have when God revealed himself.

The last trap I want to lay before you is *the danger of feeling you are indispensable.*

> There he went into a cave and spent the night.
>
> And the word of the LORD came to him: "What are you doing here, Elijah?"
>
> He replied, "I have been very zealous for the LORD God Almighty. The Israelites have rejected your covenant, broken down your altars, and put your prophets to death with the sword. I am the only one left, and now they are trying to kill me too" (vv. 9-10).

"Lord, I'm the only one left, and if they take me, what will happen to your cause?"

I wonder how many great works, founded under the direction of God, have folded because of one so-called indispensable man? I'm thinking of one Christian organization greatly used of God. It was founded by a man of faith and vision who developed it and built it, but he couldn't let go of it. Not only was he its founder and its developer, he was also its undertaker, for he buried it. It is basic to spiritual growth and usefulness that we realize no man is indispensable to God; he is only an instrument. God wants to use you. The danger is that when he does use you, you may begin to think you are the one doing it. I am convinced that periodically God removes an individual in order to convince us afresh that this is not our work but his.

A young man was dead drunk on a destroyer in Pearl Harbor the morning the Japanese air force struck. In the providence of God, his ship was not hit. Subsequent to that experience he came to know Jesus Christ as his Savior in the

"It is basic to spiritual growth and usefulness that we realize no man is indispensable to God; he is only an instrument."

> *". . . you do not measure a life by its duration. You measure it by its contribution."*

servicemen's center in Honolulu. After the war he finished college, then came to our seminary, graduated, and became a naval chaplain.

During a ministry I had in the islands, it was my privilege to have fellowship with him. What a thrill. He held three Sunday morning services in the chapel. And at each one there were more than 300 men who heard the gospel. He invited a large corps of servicemen to come home with him for dinner. After the meal, we sat around the living room, and for three hours they plied me with questions.

In spite of having to compete with first-run movies that cost just a dime, the chapel was packed to the doors for the evening service. And these young men were hearing the gospel and being taught the Word. Men from bases on the other side of the island would drive clear across the island in order to get into a Bible study taught by this chaplain.

I was scarcely back in Dallas when I received a telegram that this young man had been killed. He'd gone to Guam to dedicate a servicemen's center that he had been instrumental in starting. As the plane was taking off the edge of the runway after he had dedicated the building, it dropped into the jungles. It took three days to find the wreckage.

When I got that message, it was like being hit by a two-by-four. He left four children—all under the age of seven. Being a father of four myself, my heart went out to his wife. I sat down to write her the most difficult letter I have ever written, and yet the most instructive to me. I said, "Carol, all things work together. God has underlined that little word *together* in my mind. Not in isolation, but together for good." I thought of all the chaplains I had met, many of whom had no concern for spiritual things or the Word of God. Yet here was a man with zeal, and he was taken away. I think it was then that God began to teach me that you do not measure a life by its duration. You measure it by its contribution.

Suppose Jezebel had snuffed out the life of Elijah? It is altogether possible that this move might have galvanized those 7,000 prophets of Jehovah in the cave. Who are we to judge? No one is indispensable in God's service.

You'll remember the rest of the story. God reveals himself through various spectacular and dramatic means, but it is finally in the still, small voice that he gets through to Elijah. God wanted to teach the prophet, and you and me, that he not only speaks in the spectacular, he also speaks in silence. He not only speaks in his glory, he also speaks in the grime.

Another great man who had an effect on me was Dr. Harry Ironside, who came to our seminary on several occasions. I came to appreciate the refreshing down-to-earthness of his spiritual life. I remember asking him one day, "Dr. Ironside, what do you think of a lot of the teaching on the spiritual life?" I'll never forget his response: "I think it's wonderful, if you have a lot of time and a lot of money." It took me a long time to understand what he was saying.

Do you know the kind of spiritual life I have come to appreciate? It's the kind that works when three of your four small children are sick in one night. If spiritual living works there, that's what we need, because that's the kind of life we are living.

Have you learned the glory of the grind? To be on the mountaintop is tremendously exciting. But to be in the marketplace, to be in the office, the shop, the home, and there to live distinctively for Christ—that's what we need. That's what God offers to me and to you. But there are many traps en route, and the greater the knowledge of the enemy, the greater the potential for victory.

CONCLUSION

The saga of Elijah inevitably quickens the heartbeat of the frustrated believer. The chronicle of Kings declares, "There was never a man like Ahab, who sold himself to do evil in the eyes of the LORD, urged on by Jezebel his wife. He behaved in the vilest manner by going after idols . . ." (1 Kings 21:25, 26). In the face of the royal defiance from the throne of Israel, God planted a monumental stop sign: the prophet Elijah. His life and ministry teach the most timid of us what God can do to curtail sin when he has a willing deputy.

Elijah's initial role was confrontation with the irreverent Ahab; he sternly issued God's drought bulletin. Then, in a contrastive mood, we saw the prophet by the brook, tutored, refreshed, his faith readied for the conflict.

The Mount Carmel clash stands as the high point of Elijah's statement to the world, the vindication of the ministry of God's man. The key to this unique life is what God said to him, and what he said to man—his communication. In final dramatic contrast, Elijah's personal crises underscore his humanity and provide for us today an inside look at God's remedy for discouragement.

Elijah's stormy sojourn in Samaria stirs the thoughtful reader to action. The impact of this human thunderbolt who passionately determined to oppose wickedness and affirm the power of God stands in history as a motivation for every restless believer who is frustrated in a spiritual quagmire. He was no bionic believer; in fact, the record reveals appalling weakness, but he knew how to tap into the power line of divine energy. "Just like us," reminds James. "The prayer of a righteous man is powerful and effective."